D1474891

Live Action English

by

International Rescue Committee
2020 Hurley Way #395
Sacramento, CA 95825

Elizabeth Kuizenga Romijn
&
Contee Seely

Foreword by James J. Asher

Millennium Edition

Command Performance Language Institute
28 Hopkins Court
Berkeley, CA 94706-2512
U.S.A.
Tel: 510-524-1191
Fax: 510-527-9880
E-mail: info@cpli.net
www.cpli.net

Live Action English
is published by the
Command Performance Language Institute,
which features
Total Physical Response products
and other fine products
related to language acquisition
and teaching.

To obtain copies of *Live Action English*,
contact one of the distributors
listed inside the front cover.

Cover art by Pol (www.polanimation.com)
Other illustrations by Elizabeth Kuizenga Romijn

First edition: April, 1979 — eleventh printing: September, 1986
Revised edition: July, 1988 — third printing: September, 1990
Millennium edition: November, 1997 — fourth printing: May, 2007

Copyright © 2007, 2002, 2000, 1997, 1988, 1979 by Elizabeth Kuizenga Romijn and
Contee Seely. All rights reserved. No part of this book may be reproduced or trans-
mitted in any form or by any means, electronic or mechanical, including photocopy-
ing, recording or by any information storage and retrieval system, without permission
in writing from one of the authors.

Printed in the U.S.A.

ISBN-10: 0-929724-16-X (formerly 0-13-539453-8)
ISBN-13: 978-0-929724-16-4

CONTENTS

FOREWORD

In 20 years of research we have found that when students respond with appropriate actions to commands, their learning is far more efficient and their involvement fuller than if they do not move. In English, for example, it is not enough for students to understand the meaning of *stand up* and *sit down*. They must construct their own reality by physically standing when they hear "stand up" and sitting when they hear "sit down." The lessons in this book are based, first and foremost, on this principle (Secondarily they are based on Gouin's discovery that series help the memory.).

The authors do not assume that the students who use this book know no English. Nor do they assume that the instructor will do nothing more than use the material here presented. With students who are beginning at the lowest levels, we have discovered that an optimal format is for them to start by silently listening to directions in the target language and responding with appropriate actions. Speaking from students is delayed until comprehension has been thoroughly internalized. Eventually, as comprehension of the target language expands and expands, talk will spontaneously appear. Of course, like infants learning their first language, when speech appears, there will be many distortions. But gradually, in time, with the skillful coaching of the instructor, student speech will shape itself in the direction of the native speaker. The procedures recommended in this book are one well-developed way to provide this coaching and will also help students who have not had the good fortune to begin their language learning with this exciting approach.

The publication of this book is especially welcome, as it is the first student text that makes use of Total Physical Response to be published in the English-speaking world.

James J. Asher
February, 1979

iv

INTRODUCTION

This book consists of 67 series of commands which are actually put into action by every member of a class, thereby creating live situations. It is not a complete course. However, it will combine extremely well with all sorts of other materials at the beginning and intermediate levels. It is particularly well-suited to the multi-level class, because students at both levels—and often advanced students too—learn with full involvement in every series.

It is also excellent for open-enrollment classes for adults, because it provides a new set of vocabulary words each class session (or couple of sessions) on which can be based the same grammar lesson or lessons time after time. The regular students never feel that the class is at all repetitive, because the context is always new. However, newcomers, or people who cannot get to every class session, can pick up wherever you are on the day they come, because the lessons are not based on the assumption that the vocabulary is already understood; the vocabulary is new and learned thoroughly by everyone in the class, each day, before any grammar points are tackled. (See "Creative Adaptations," p. xx, nos. 1 and 2.) The people who do come to each session learn faster, because they practice the same points again and again in each context, thus acquiring these structures in a way that more closely approximates first language acquisition than do most classroom activities.

FOR TEACHERS NEW TO TPR. Some groups or teachers are not accustomed to working in the manner in which these series are most profitably used. So, although the lessons may be used in any order, we recommend that you start with some of the simpler, briefer, more obvious ones. The first 18 lessons are especially appropriate for this purpose.

Some teachers who are new to this approach will find certain things about the classroom procedures unusual and a little uncomfortable at first. During the presentation (step 2, "Procedures," p. xii) the students remain silent while listening and watching the action. This silence can seem strange but is necessary for good hearing and comprehension and subsequent pronunciation. In the final step (the 7th, pp. xv and xvi) all the students practice in a tremendous babble that often appears chaotic but is actually very efficient, allowing each student far more opportunity for real communication than in the usual language class. Another unusual aspect is the emotional expression, exaggerated action and theatrical drama required of the instructor.

HISTORICAL BASIS. The approach on which this book is based has its roots in the work of Frenchman François Gouin, Englishman Harold E. Palmer and American James J. Asher. Gouin published *L'art d'enseigner et d'étudier les langues*[1] in 1880. He gave a detailed description of the use of series without mak-

---

[1]Paris: Librairie Fischbacher; English translation by H. Swan and V. Bétis, *The Art of Teaching and Studying Languages*, London: Philip, 1892.

v

ing mention of enacting them. In Palmer's *English through Actions*[2] debt was paid to Gouin and action was brought into prominence. Asher (who wrote the foreword to this book) has done nearly 30 years of research which has clearly established the high effectiveness of Total Physical Response with students of all ages. A psychologist at San José State University, he has published numerous articles describing his research and a book entitled *Learning Another Language Through Actions: The Complete Teacher's Guidebook*,[3] as well as producing several films (now available as videos from Sky Oaks Productions) which demonstrate this approach.

THE BASICS OF TPR. Briefly, Asher's approach is based on these three fundaments of language instruction:
   • Understanding the spoken language should precede speaking.
   • Understanding should be developed through movements of the student's body, especially (but not only) in response to imperatives.
   • Speaking should not be encouraged until the student is ready for it.[4]

Asher feels that most approaches cause stress and frustration by requiring students to speak before they are ready to. Responding physically to commands is an extremely efficient way to achieve readiness to speak *without causing stress or frustration.*

ADVANTAGES OF SERIES. Among the many advantages of using series in language acquisition/learning are the following: (1) Series facilitate remembering, as Gouin noted. Recent psychological studies have compared the memorization of lists of non-sequential items with logically connected sequences. Such studies have born out Gouin's observations of a century ago. (2) Series provide a context for meaning. (3) Series are life-like situations. The more life-like the situation, the more engaging and motivating it is. (4) While series are good for learning lots of things, they are especially good for expanding students' repertoires of verbs.

VOCATIONAL ADVANTAGE OF IMPERATIVES. There is an additional advantage to sequences of imperatives for ESL students who have jobs or expect to get them soon. Commands are used with great frequency in most, if not all, job areas. A research project done in Texas[5] showed that in over 4,000 oral samples of language on the job *a full 40% involved imperatives!* The samples were gathered from 12 diverse fields of work, including business, welding, health, food service and auto mechanics. The same study also indicated that *most verbs are useful in all vocations,* whereas nouns tend to be specific to a particular occupation. These findings strongly suggest that learning series of commands is highly useful to students involved in a variety of activities.

---

[2]Co-authored by his daughter, Dorothée Palmer, Tokyo: Institute of Research in Language Teaching, 1925; slightly revised later edition: London: Longman, 1959.
[3]Los Gatos, Calif.: Sky Oaks Productions, 5th ed., 1996.
[4]Ibid., page 2-4.
[5]In 1979-80 by the Resource Development Institute of Austin, under the direction of Mary Galvan.

PUBLISHING HISTORY. *Live Action English* was first published in 1979. To our amazement, it has enjoyed 15 printings, and about 52,000 copies are now in print. Two years after the initial publication in the United States, a British edition appeared (Oxford: Pergamon; currently out of print.) The materials in *Live Action English* were developed in the classroom in work with adult learners of English and, in many cases, Spanish. Much to our surprise again, the English version has been widely used with elementary and secondary school and college students as well as with adults. It has been used successfully with students of many and diverse nationalities all over the world—in the U.S., Canada, China, Korea, Thailand, Japan, the Philippines, Indonesia, Australia, Brazil, most of Spanish America, Spain, France, Germany, Austria, the U.K., Italy, Israel, Morocco, Nigeria and many other areas—with remarkable enthusiasm. Many of the series have also been translated and used with American students who were learning Spanish, French, German, Italian, Japanese, Finnish and other languages—with the same enthusiasm.

ADDITIONAL *LIVE ACTION* MATERIALS. In 1985 a set of two *Live Action English Cassettes* was produced. In 2000 a revised set was recorded by Elizabeth Kuizenga Romijn. Versions of the book in Spanish (*¡Viva la acción!*), French (*Vive l'action!*), German (*Lernt aktiv!*), Italian (*Viva l'azione!*) and Japanese (*Iki Iki Nihongo*) are also available from distributors.

Action English Pictures, with illustrations by former English student Noriko Takahashi and text by Maxine Frauman-Prickel (Hayward, Calif.: Alemany Press, 1985; now available from Alta Book Center (1999 printing)), is based directly on *Live Action English*. It consists of 66 duplicatable picture lessons—39 of which are the very same series which are in *Live Action English*, but without words. There is a picture for each line of text in the included *Live Action English* lessons. (See illustration on last page, and see p. 73 for a complete list of the lessons which are in both books.)

TPR Is More Than Commands—At All Levels by Contee Seely and Elizabeth Kuizenga Romijn (Berkeley, California: Command Performance, 1995; 2nd edition, 1998; see inside back cover) shows how to use the *Live Action* series to teach numerous features of any language.

The first TPR computer program ever, the CD-ROM *Live Action English Interactive*, was released in 2000. It was created by ESL teacher and software developer Larry Statan with CALL consultation from Elizabeth Hanson-Smith and Robert Wachman and contains nine units from this book as well as three new ones written by the authors and Statan especially for this multimedia program. (See the final page of this book for details.)

FIVE NEW LESSONS. The revised edition (1988) featured two new lessons. On page 23 "A Wrinkled Shirt" replaced "A Balloon Trick." The trick, which involved sticking straight pins in a balloon without popping it, was found to work only with high quality balloons which may not be available to all users of the book. The other new lesson was "Taking a Hike," on page 65—a favorite sequence in a great variety of classes for many years.

This Millennium Edition replaces "Stop! Thief!" on page 20 with "Playing a Cassette," "Hungry Bugs" on page 29 with "Hiccups," and "Fight" on page 42 with "Giving Directions." Although the replaced lessons contained important vocabulary for learners of English, we feel that because of their violent nature, there are more appropriate ways to present this language than through the use of the imperative. The three new lessons involve vocabulary of useful life skills.

SIMILAR MATERIALS. Several books have appeared which are similar to *Live Action English* in that they consist of series of actions:

1. *The Children's Response* by Caroline Linse (Hayward, Calif.: Alemany Press, 1983) contains 60 English series deftly designed for elementary school children. (currently out of print)

2. *Actionlogues* by Joanne "Jody" Klopp (Los Gatos, Calif.: Sky Oaks Productions, 1985) presents 25 series with a photograph for each line—available in Spanish, German and French only; cassettes available in all three languages.

3. *Action Sequence Stories* by Constance Williams (Menlo Park, Calif.: Williams and Williams, 1987 and 1988; currently available from Ballard & Tighe, 480 Atlas St., Brea, CA 92621; phone: (800) 321-4322) consists of two kits of materials, each of which includes 50 six-line command sequences. Spanish, English, French, German and Italian versions of the sequences are available.

4. *English Operations* by Gayle Nelson and Thomas Winters (Brattleboro, VT: Pro Lingua, 1993) has 55 everyday sequences in English. This is a revised and expanded edition of *ESL Operations*, published by Newbury House in 1980.

5. *Picture It!: Sequences for Conversation* (Tokyo: International Communications, 1978; New York: Regents, 1981; currently available from Pearson Education) has 60 eight-line, fully-illustrated sequences which are in a variety of English tenses and were not intended to be acted out. While only a handful are in the imperative, all can be done with action and adapted to the imperative.

6. *Listen and Act* by Dale Griffee (Tucson: Lingual House, 1982) contains "mini-drama" sequences in which a "director" gives commands to "actors" and "actresses" who perform the actions.

7. *English for Everyday Activities: A Picture Process Dictionary* by Lawrence J. Zwier (Hong Kong: Asia-Pacific Press Holdings; North American edition: Syracuse, NY: New Readers Press, 1999) presents 61 chapters of one sequence (or in some cases more than one) in simple present or simple past (and in one case in simple future). There is a color drawing for every action. A supplementary activity book is available, as are an audiotape and an activity book that accompanies the tape.

ACKNOWLEDGMENTS

We deeply appreciate the suggestions of **Berty Segal** and **Ruth Cathcart** which we have incorporated into the introductory sections of all versions of this book. We also wish to thank **Maggie Seely, Jaap Romijn, Eduardo Hernández-Chávez, Ken Beck, Judy Winn-Bell Olsen, Helen Valdez, Helen McCully, Patricia Helton** and **James Asher** for their constant encouragement in the writing of the original English version. "Hiccups" (p. 29) is an adaptation of a Spanish "audio-motor unit" in a personal communication from **Theodore Kalivoda** in 1974. We are grateful, too, to **Roberta MacFarlane, Nick Kremer** and **Mary Galvan** for information on research dealing with on-the-job language (p. *vi*). We would like to thank **Tamara Romijn** and **Talmadge Heath** for assistance in the production of the revised English edition. Special thanks go to **Robert Dawson** and **John Seely** for providing extra voices on the original *Live Action English Cassettes*. Our greatest thanks go to **OUR STUDENTS**, who have been our inspiration over the last 26 years. These materials have grown and developed in direct response to their joy and enthusiasm in learning this way. We wish you the same enthusiasm and joy.

THE AUTHORS INVITE YOU

You are welcome to observe the authors using these materials in their language classes in the San Francisco Bay Area.

Elizabeth Kuizenga Romijn grew up in Ann Arbor, Michigan. She received a B.A. in Linguistics from the University of California in Berkeley in 1969 and began teaching ESL that fall for the Mission Campus of City College of San Francisco, where she can still be found today. In 1983 she received an M.A. in Linguistics-ESL from San José State University. She is the author of *Puppies or Poppies: ESL Bingo*, a teacher's resource book. With Contee Seely she is co-author of *TPR Is More Than Commands—At All Levels* (see inside back cover for both books). She has presented teacher workshops on TPR and multi-level ESL throughout California. She has two daughters, Rebecca Romijn Stamos and Tamara Romijn, and lives in Richmond, California. Call Contee Seely at (510) 524-1191 for times and locations of Elizabeth's classes.

Contee Seely graduated from Princeton University in 1961. He has taught English to adult speakers of other languages in Ecuador, Peru, Chile and the United States and has also taught Spanish in high school and to adults (including Peace Corps trainees) in the U.S. and at Vista College in Berkeley. With Elizabeth Romijn he is co-author of *TPR Is More Than Commands—At All Levels* and, with Blaine Ray, of *Fluency Through TPR Storytelling* (see inside back cover for both books). Currently he teaches Spanish for the Neighborhood Centers Adult School in the Oakland public schools (in the evening). In 1989 he received the Excellence in Teaching Award presented by the California Council for Adult Education. He is publisher at the Command Performance Language Institute in Berkeley and gives teacher training workshops at all levels on TPR and Blaine Ray's TPR Storytelling (recommended by Prof. James J. Asher). You can reach Contee at (510) 524-1191. He and his wife Maggie have a son, Michael, and a daughter, Christina.

ix

GENERAL PROCEDURES FOR
ENACTING EACH SERIES

> The teacher's skill [lies] in presenting
> experiences in such a way that the student
> [is] bound to succeed.
> Keith Johnstone
> *Impro: Improvisation and the Theatre*

These procedures are intended to be used with adults, with college students and with secondary school students. However, we recognize that there are numerous ways to present these lessons. Some of the other ways are described in Chapter 2 of *TPR Is More Than Commands—At All Levels* (Seely and Romijn, 1995). One of these ways is given below on pages *xviii* and *xix*. It is the way that Berty Segal Cook (a.k.a. Berty Segal) suggests for use with elementary and secondary school classes. The procedures that follow are the ones that we have used with our beginning students. With more advanced students we have varied the order of the steps in order to de-emphasize the receptive stages.

The **final objective** of these procedures is for each student to be able to demonstrate his/her adequate pronunciation and comprehension of the language of the series at hand by telling another student to perform it and, conversely, to be able to respond physically to another person's delivery of the commands. The first six of the following steps are used as **a method of preparing students to be ready to work effectively and independently in the seventh and final step:**

A. RECEPTIVE STAGE: LISTENING

 1. Setting up (1-2 minutes)

 2. Initial demonstration of series (1-2 minutes)

 3. Group live action (2-3 minutes)

B. RECEPTIVE STAGE: READING (AND SOME WRITING)

 4. Written copy (2-10 minutes, depending on whether or not students must copy it and also on the writing skills and age level of the students)

C. EXPRESSIVE STAGE: SPEAKING

 5. Oral repetition and question/answer period (5-10 minutes)

 6. Student(s) speaking/other person responding (5-10 minutes)

 7. Students all working in pairs (5-15 minutes)

The first six steps are only suggestions and can be changed or alternated. You may experiment and **do whatever you find necessary to properly prepare students for step 7.**

If you ever run out of time during a class session, start at the beginning again at the next session. The review will go faster and make things easier for everybody.

A detailed description of each of the suggested procedures follows.

BEFOREHAND—PREPARING REALIA

These lessons are specifically intended to be used with props. If you have never used props before, you may question the value of spending the time to gather and prepare them. We have found that they are invaluable not only as a source of fun but as an aid to comprehension and retention. See the list of props necessary for each lesson on pp. 69-73, and assemble the props you need before you begin working on a particular series. If you can't manage to come up with an appropriate prop, you can sometimes improvise by using something similar in shape and size. (Regarding props see also *The Command Book* by Stephen Silvers (Los Gatos, Calif.: Sky Oaks Productions, 1988).)

The presentation should be realistic and obvious. For younger students and lower level students of all ages, this is especially true, so that the language will really be about a "happening" which is affecting the students' muscles and their senses. Totally experiencing the situation makes a strong impression and connects the words to something real, making learning much easier, more effective and more enjoyable for any student.

Props will be just one of various ways in which you will make meaning clear to the students. Go over the series, thinking about just how you will present each bit of the series to the particular class you intend to use it with. Some groups will require a more thorough presentation than others. Certain items may require greater or less attention with some classes—due to the level of the class or to similarities and differences between the first language of the learners and English.

A. RECEPTIVE STAGE: LISTENING

1. SETTING UP and Working Into the Series

Set up your situation in front of the students' eyes—as they are assembling at the beginning of class, or as they are finishing up some other work, or even with their full attention. For some series this will only involve laying out some props. Sometimes you can improvise with whatever is available. For example, in "Bank" (p. 35) the rungs in the back of a chair or a Venetian blind may serve as the teller's window. Or an aisle can be a city street or a diving board. In other series you may need an illustration of a certain room or scene (commercially produced, cut from a magazine, or simply drawn by a student or yourself on the board), such as the downtown street in "Shopping for a New Coat" (p. 11), the phone booth in "Pay Phone" (p. 30) or the fireplace in "Building a Fire" (p. 47). In still others, such as "Doctor's Appointment" (p. 59) and "Haircut" (p. 43), you'll need to recruit some students for minor roles and introduce them as the receptionist, the nurse, the doctor, the barber, etc.

Talk about what you are doing in order to work into the series naturally and casually. For example, for "Washing Your Hands" (p. 1) you might make remarks such as: "Now I'm going to wash my hands" or "Oh, look at this; my hands are dirty" (maybe they really are, from something else you've been doing). Then, as you set out each object, ask if anyone knows its name. Hold up the soap and ask, "What do you call this?" and repeat with the towel and the faucet. If anyone would understand the words *sink* and *bathroom*, indicate that you are in the bathroom or at the sink. If your class is small, you may even go to a real sink for the initial demonstration.

2. INITIAL DEMONSTRATION OF SERIES

Now ask the class not to talk any more: "Don't talk; don't repeat; only look and listen." *It is essential that everyone be paying attention to the action now.*

If you have a student who might understand some or all of the commands in the series, or an aide or a visitor, have that person respond physically to your reading (with *loads* of expression!) of the series. If no such person is available, demonstrate the action yourself the first time. Take plenty of time to make sure each action is fully understood. If you're not sure that everyone followed it, repeat it once or twice, using the same "performer" again, or a new one each time. You or the performer(s) may have to use pantomime for some actions.

3. GROUP LIVE ACTION

Thank your performer and address the entire class with: "Now *you're* going to wash *your* hands." You might even begin with: "Look at *your* hands! They're dirty! Ugh! Turn on the water," etc.

You will probably have to ask again that no one repeat or talk at all during this time. Now they are to respond physically to the imperatives, experiencing the words as real communication, learning with their muscles, *living* the language. Usually not every person has every object in the series. So they can pantomime the actions which they cannot actually perform. Many people need some prodding at this point. If someone does not turn the water on, you might hand that person the faucet and repeat, "Please turn on the water." If some people don't wash their hands, you might ask, "Where's your soap?" If some people say they don't need to do these things because they already understand them, tell them that although understanding is of course necessary, it's not enough, that they will *remember* the words much better if they *experience* them.

Some adults may even be a little insulted at first, feeling that these little pantomimes are childish. However, we have rarely seen any students continue to feel this way after one lesson, because they realize very quickly how much they are learning and how easily. Even advanced students learn some new words and usages in most series.

Note especially: It is advisable to go through step 3 several times on different occasions (thereby allowing students to thoroughly internalize the series) before they read it and produce it orally. The lower the level of the class, the more times it is necessary to do this.

B. RECEPTIVE STAGE: READING (AND SOME WRITING)

The first three steps in the procedures are the listening or receptive stage. Step 4 is reading and writing. Students generally should not proceed to reading or writing until they are ready for the speaking or expressive stage, which is steps 5 to 7. *There are two keys to readiness to proceed*:

1. Unhesitating facility in responding physically to the commands

2. The ability to repeat easily after the teacher

4. WRITTEN COPY

When all the students can respond physically without hesitation to the lesson, display a large copy of it. You may put it on a reusable poster or on the chalkboard, or you may use an overhead projector. *Make sure the lesson is easy to read from anywhere in the classroom.* Have all the students copy the entire lesson in their notebooks. In addition to or instead of using the large copy, you may have each student use a copy of the textbook. Copying the lesson can be useful in itself, especially for younger and low-level students. This is an early-stage reading and writing exercise.

After everyone has a copy, read it to them while they listen and follow only. *Do not have them repeat after you during this first reading.* Then ask if they have any questions about the meaning. *Try to answer these questions with motions rather than translations.*

Some students panic at the sight of written words, especially in English, and fail to realize that these are the same words that they have just understood aurally and have responded to appropriately. This would need to be brought to their attention, even if it means your going through the actions again each time you read or point to a line.

PLEASE NOTE: The large display copy is very useful from this point on, because it allows you to point out individual words and phrases. It also helps by keeping the students in touch with the teacher or with their partners instead of buried in their papers or books.

C. EXPRESSIVE STAGE: SPEAKING

5. ORAL REPETITION and QUESTION AND ANSWER PERIOD

Next have the students repeat each line after you, taking plenty of time to go over individual words which are particularly difficult to pronounce or understand. *Make sure every student can hear your pronunciation fully.* If s/he can't, s/he won't be able to pronounce well.

If the class is really struggling to pronounce, you should return to the receptive stage and do more individual (step 2) and group (step 3) live action before getting them to repeat after you again. Or, this may be an indication that the group is at too low a level to deal with the particular sequence you are doing with them. In this case, look at the suggestions in the section entitled "Using This Book with Very Low Beginners" on page *xvii*.

Give the students some extra time to look over the series and ask more questions. This might also be a good time to point out some minimal pairs— soap/soup, wash/watch—and do some work on these.

6. STUDENT(S) SPEAKING/OTHER PERSON RESPONDING

Now ask for a volunteer, or choose a student, to tell *you* to do the entire series. Or, since each line is numbered, assign several individuals a line or two by number. If you only take volunteers at this point, probably some students will never read, so it is best to *choose* readers, at least sometimes.

This is a good opportunity for you to hear pronunciation problems. Generally, if one student has a problem pronouncing a certain word or phrase, there are others too, and this means more group practice is needed. Make sure the students hear well. This is the first essential for good pronunciation.

Next you may want to have one student do the physical responses in front of the class or at his or her desk as another student reads. There may be a new student or less responsive student who doesn't seem to be following the language. This is a good time to find out if this is just shyness, or confusion about the new method, or if indeed s/he doesn't understand what is being said. Whatever the problem is, it can probably be ironed out as that student follows the other's commands, with some encouraging prompting from you.

You may want to have more students tell you or the whole class to do the series. Remember that what you're doing is preparing them to do the series unsupervised. Whether or not you go on or repeat steps 5 and/or 6 a few times depends on how the students are sounding and responding.

7. STUDENTS ALL WORKING IN PAIRS

When you feel that the students are clear enough on the language of the series (comprehending, responding, pronouncing), ask them to work in pairs or threes, one telling (or reading) and the other(s) listening and responding physically. In doing so, each student will experience the power of actually speaking English and having his or her commands acted upon by another person, thus truly communicating in English about something which is actually occurring.

You may form the groups yourself to allow greater learning opportunities, or you may let the class form its own pairs or threes. Make sure everyone has a partner (or partners).

This also frees the instructor to work individually with students. You can evaluate the lesson, your presentation of it, the students' grasp of it and individual progress. Your job now changes from director to aide. Go around the room listening, helping, correcting, approving, encouraging reluctant students to practice ("for your memory"). Make sure every student goes through the series at least twice—once telling, once responding (except for students who are not yet ready to speak; they should be paired with more advanced students and should respond only). More advanced students, or those who have done this series before, can be encouraged to try it without looking at the copy. Answer questions people may have been too shy to ask before the group.

It is helpful to get a student who is used to working this way to break in a new student. However, occasionally new students may need to have *you* work individually with them, physically going through the entire series, as an example of the way you mean for them to work.

Usually some students will need more guidance than others on how to use this time. People who spend the whole time recopying the lesson or looking up and translating words may be doing so simply because they don't know what else to do. Point out that these are things that can be done at home, and that this time is basically for oral practice and realistic response.

However, do let the students follow their own impulses. You will be surprised at the large variety of things different people will work on at this time. The more freedom you give them, the more that will happen. Furthermore, some of the activities that may seem irrelevant or even counterproductive to you may in fact be serving some important purpose for the students involved. Even simply recopying may be as important as anything else to a student illiterate in his or her native language and as much as s/he can handle on a particular occasion. Different people have different ways of learning, of fixing things in their minds, and of checking their own comprehension and mastery of what has just transpired. Give them enough time to tie up the loose ends as they see them. And keep your eyes and ears open. Your sensitivity to the situation can help some individuals immensely and can help you know how to deal better with other series. When the students finish practicing, call them to order and congratulate them on doing a good job. You may have the class repeat difficult items after you—or the whole series—one last time.

You may review a series at any time. Generally you will find retention notably better than with other types of exercises. And the review will improve it even more.

These procedures are useful, with minor adaptations, to prepare students to do other kinds of work in pairs, as well as series. Many teachers have been unsuccessful in their previous attempts at having students work in pairs. The main source of difficulty is that the students have not been adequately prepared. Using the above procedures, students *are* properly prepared.

USING THIS BOOK WITH
VERY LOW BEGINNERS

With very new learners of English, we suggest you *not* begin by using the full procedures given on pages *x* to *xvi*. By "very low beginners" we mean learners who are *really new* to English, who have virtually no experience of any kind with English. Some such learners may have no familiarity with the Latin alphabet or any system of writing. Very low beginners may need to hear and experience English in a meaningful context for a considerable period of time before they are encouraged to speak it at all.

Here are some ways to ease new learners into English:

1. Do only the first three steps of the procedures, going over numerous series several times each before you ever encourage the learners to say anything in any series. This way they will internalize the material very thoroughly before speaking it and will be very comfortable with it when they finally do say it.

2. Simplify the series considerably. See #2 in "Creative Adaptations" on page *xx*.

3. Choose some of the simpler commands from various series and work on these for some time with the students listening and responding physically. You can use recombinations by using different nouns with whatever verbs you choose, as in #5 on page *xxi*.

4. Devise and do *very* brief action dialogs. See page *xxii*, #10. Be sure every student is adequately prepared before s/he does a dialog on her/his own. This means s/he (a) has experienced it before her/his eyes in a meaningful context many times and (b) has heard good, natural (but *not* fast) pronunciation several times for imitation and has heard it very well.

1. Unwrap the cheese.

2. Put it on the cutting board.

3. Pick up the knife.

See pp. *xviii* and *xix* regarding the use of the above illustrations.

(based on "Cheese," p. 4)

USING THIS BOOK WITH ELEMENTARY
AND SECONDARY SCHOOL STUDENTS

World-renowned TPR author and teacher trainer Berty Segal Cook (a.k.a. Berty Segal) recommends the following procedures for elementary (from third grade up) and secondary school classes:

1. The teacher reads the sequence or series aloud line by line with appropriate feeling as s/he acts it out along with two or three students. The rest of the class observes.

2. S/he reads it aloud again and models it again, this time as the entire class acts it out along with her/him.

3. One of the following is done:
    a. Secondary school. The teacher places before the class a large copy of the sequence which has been prepared beforehand. This large copy must be easily readable from every student's seat. Preferably it is written on a poster-sized sheet so it can be reused, though it may be written on the chalkboard.
    b. Elementary school. Students are each given a book (or one book for each two students to share) which contains the series; if books are not available, they are given a photocopy of the sequence on paper from which to write out their own copy. The reason that elementary school students are given books or papers is that it is difficult for many of them to correctly copy words from the wall or the chalkboard.

4. The class reads the entire series *in chorus* together with the teacher.

5. Every student is given a rubber band or a clip and a large sheet of paper, at least 11" by 17" (28 x 43 cm.), preferably 18" by 24" (45 x 61 cm.) or even larger. Lined paper is best for this exercise.

6. Each student copies each line of the series in large writing onto her/his large sheet, numbering each line in order.

7. Each student now draws a picture at the end of each line of the sequence to represent the action of the line. Generally speaking, the larger the paper, the easier it is for students to make these drawings. There is no need for the drawings to be fine. Each student will use her or his own drawings a little later. When this step is completed, there are a number, a sentence and a drawing on each line of each student's paper. (See **illustration** at the bottom of p. *xvii*)

PAIR WORK: Steps 8-15 are generally done with the students working in pairs. Preferably they change partners several times as they go through these steps.

8. One student reads each line of the series to her or his partner, pausing between lines for the partner to perform the action. Then the actor becomes the reader and vice versa.

9. Each student cuts her/his paper into strips, one line per strip, with number, sentence and drawing.

10. Each student mixes up her/his strips and then puts her/his rubber band or clip on the whole set to hold it together.

The following four exercises (11-14) are especially useful for younger students who need to learn the skill of sequencing.

11. Every student finds a new partner. Each pair of students has two sets of strips. They choose one of the sets and put the strips in order.

12. The students mix up those strips again and get new partners. Then the teacher tells the students to fold the numbers back so that they cannot be seen. Each pair of students puts one set of strips in order, this time without the help of the numbers.

13. The students change partners again. Then they cut off the pictures with scissors and mix them up. After that they put the pictures in their proper sequence and clip or bind the set of pictures together.

14. After forming new pairs, students (now without numbers or pictures as clues) read the text on their strips to each other in order, each one following and checking her or his partner's reading and sequencing.

15. After changing partners once more, each student produces orally the whole series in order, using her/his own pictures as cues while the partner listens, performs the commands and helps if necessary. (The simultaneous oral production and performance of the commands by everyone can cause discipline problems in some classes. If so, omit the performance of the commands.)

16. Finally, working individually again, on a regular-sized sheet of paper each student writes out the entire series in order, using the pictures as cues.

Note that in this process students become thoroughly familiar with the series as they listen, read, copy, speak and write. You shouldn't expect first- and second-grade second language learners to go through this entire process, because they are generally not well enough founded in reading and writing in their *first language* to start dealing with reading and writing in another language. It is best to concentrate on aural/oral language with these younger students. They would do only the steps in the receptive stage (pp. *xi* to *xiii*, or numbers 1 and 2 above), performing the commands. These steps can be repeated a number of times and may be done on several different days. First- and second-graders may also make drawings for the commands. If they do, they can then cut each drawing off of the paper, mix up their drawings and sequence them. Those who are able to may be invited to give commands without being required to produce them all. In any event the comprehensible input will eventually bring about production, just as it does in their first language.

Children whose first language is English and students in bilingual classes, up through the 6th grade (age 11-12), also enjoy and profit from the series in *Live Action English*. They are useful in the early stages of the development of reading and writing skills. Specifically, they are helpful in the learning of sequencing and chronological narration. They are also good for teaching and checking on the skill of following directions, as Caroline Linse points out in *The Children's Response* (see #1 on p. *viii*). In addition, they can form the basis for language experience approach (LEA) stories (stories told by students about their own experiences and written down by a teacher) and provide a stimulus for creative writing.

If you are teaching elementary school children, you will probably want to be somewhat selective in choosing which lessons in *Live Action English* you use. Some will work better if you adapt or simplify them to fit the level.

CREATIVE ADAPTATIONS

To a much greater degree than most material, these lessons offer taking-off points for creative use of the vocabulary they contain.

We urge you to refer to our book *TPR is More Than Commands—At All Levels* (Berkeley, Calif.: Command Performance Language Institute, 1995; see inside back cover) for many ideas for the creative use of these lessons. Chapters 2, 3, 5, 6 and 7 of that book contain sections written specifically to demonstrate adaptations of the series in this book for the purpose of helping students to acquire a variety of features of their new language. These chapters include dialogs, conversations, role-playing, mini-series, fluency practice, TPR dictation, written exercises and quizzes, pronunciation and listening discrimination exercises, and detailed descriptions of how to introduce and practice eight different English verb tenses, indefinite and negative pronouns, and possessive adjectives—all based on the vocabulary of the series in *Live Action English*.

Here are some examples of the kinds of things the series can be used for:

1. Verb-form practice in present, past and future. For instance, "A Glass of Milk" (p. 12) would go like this in the past: First the teacher or a student does all the actions in silence or in response to someone's commands, while the (other) students watch. Then the person who has done the actions says, "I poured myself a glass of milk. I spilled some of it on the table...." Then all the students repeat the words after the teacher, with emphasis on the past forms. And finally all the students go through this in pairs or threes, one person at a time acting, then speaking to the other(s). In present continuous you say, "I'm pouring myself a glass of milk...." and in "*going to* future," "I'm going to pour myself a glass of milk." In all cases the actions are done at the appropriate time in relation to the words spoken. Time expressions may be taught and included: *first, then, after that, finally, now, right now....* Virtually the same process may be used in different persons—*you, he, she, we, you* (plural), *they*—with the proper persons performing. For all of these except *you* (singular) and *we*, groups of 3 or 4 are needed. (See Chapter 5 of *TPR is More Than Commands—At All Levels* for a much more detailed description of how to proceed in eight English verb tenses.)

2. For raw beginners, some of the series can be shortened. For example, "Changing a Light Bulb" (p. 32) may become:

   1. Turn on the light. It's burned out!
   2. Go get a new one.
   3. Unscrew the old bulb.
   4. Screw the new one in.
   5. Turn it on. It works!

3. The teacher asks the students questions which are about themselves or otherwise of interest, using the vocabulary of the lesson in whatever tense(s) desired.

4. Students ask questions of the teacher and of other students, using vocabulary from the lesson. Sometimes you may wish to ask them to practice a particular tense.

5. Use the same commands but with different contexts, different objects. For instance, using "Getting Home" (p. 3) as your take-off point, tell people to:

> Go downtown. (Use a picture.)
>
> Walk (or go) downstairs.
>
> Take out your pencil.
>
> Put it in your pocket.
>
> Unlock the window.
>
> Put your pen away.
>
> Turn the knob on the T.V.
>
> Open your mouth.
>
> Close it.
>
> Lock the car. (Use picture.)
>
> Turn on the radio.

Then get the students to tell you and other students to do different things, using the same verbs. It is often useful to write the verbs with some possible nouns to combine them with on the blackboard to stimulate creative use by students and to get them to lift their heads. You can use all the verbs in the series in your list or just select certain ones. Five to ten is a good working set. For example:

go (to)	door
walk (to)	padlock
unlock	outside
turn	cupboard
lock	
close	downstairs
open	[and so on]

Sentences created may be, for instance: "Unlock the cupboard," "Open the cupboard," "Walk outside"... Students may help you choose nouns for the list and may of course use other nouns while practicing.

6. Along the same lines as #5 above, improvise entire new situations, using much vocabulary from series already enacted. As you do this, some new vocabulary often emerges. As long as the meaning of it is demonstrable, this will cause no problem. In fact, some people will pick some of it up right away. The scenario that develops may be very ordinary and calm or extravagant and wild. You may do the usual kind of work with any of these improvised series or you can drop them and go on to other things. Students may also improvise their own series. Or they may write them down for subsequent use (perhaps after correction). You may too.

7. Students (and teacher) can write mini-plays for performance, involving other material as well as commands. After a number of series have been enacted by students, they will be accustomed to using English with live action, and mini-plays come more easily. The higher the level of the group, the easier it will be for them to create their own skits.

8. The non-verb vocabulary of a series may also be focused on with commands. For example, from "Scrambled Eggs" (p. 34) you or your students can produce:

> Throw me an *egg*.
> Put the *egg beater* away.
> Pass the *salt* please.
> Pour *a little milk* in the *pan*.
> Go get a *dry* towel.

9. You may write your own series to suit the particular needs or environment of your students. Vocational ESL classes, for instance, have specialized vocabulary which can be taught most effectively using this approach. (See p. *vi* regarding the use of the imperative at jobs.)

10. Very brief action dialogs (2-6 lines) may be written and enacted after adequate preparation (see "General Procedures," pp. *x* to *xvi*). Action dialogs are any dialogs with related actions and words. They are one of the basic types of TPR exercises. (See Chapter 2 of *TPR is More Than Commands—At All Levels*.) For example:

> 1 - Will you scratch my back?
> 2 - Sure, but *first* you scratch *my* back.
> *Then* I'll scratch *your* back.
> 1 - O.K.

Try this one and you'll see how much fun these little dialogs can be.

WASHING YOUR HANDS

1. You're going to wash your hands.

2. Turn on the water.

3. Pick up the soap.

4. Wash your hands.

5. Put the soap down.

6. Rinse your hands.

7. Turn off the water.

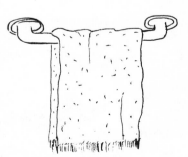

8. Pick up the towel.

9. Dry your hands.

10. Put the towel on the towel rack.

CANDLE

1. Put the candle in the candle holder.

2. Take out your matches.

3. Tear out a match.

4. Light the match.

5. Light the candle.

6. Blow out the match.

7. Throw it away.

8. Put the matches away.

9. Look at the candle.

10. Smell it.

11. Blow it out.

12. Feel it. Is it hot or cold?

GETTING HOME

1. Go home.

2. Walk upstairs.

3. Take out your key.

4. Put it in the keyhole.

5. Unlock the door.

6. Put the key away.

7. Turn the doorknob.

8. Open the door.

9. Go in.

10. Close the door.

11. Lock it.

12. Turn on the light.

13. Sit down and rest.

CHEESE

1. Unwrap the cheese.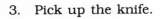

2. Put it on the cutting board.

3. Pick up the knife.

4. Cut a little piece of cheese.

5. Try it.

6. Cut another piece.

7. Eat it.

8. Cut a big piece.

9. Take a bite.

10. Chew it up and swallow it.

11. Take another bite.

12. Eat it all.

13. Wrap up the rest of the cheese.

BALLOON

1. You're going to play with a balloon.

2. Stretch the balloon.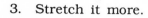

3. Stretch it more.

4. Let go of one end.

5. Blow up the balloon.

6. Don't tie it.

7. Let the air out slowly.

8. Watch the balloon shrink.

9. Blow it up again.

10. Squeeze it but don't pop it.

11. Let go of it and watch it fly.

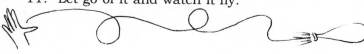

CHEWING GUM

1. Go to the store.

2. Buy a pack of gum.

3. Open the pack.

4. Take out a piece of gum.

5. Unwrap it.

6. Put it in your mouth.

7. Chew it.

8. Don't swallow it.

9. Take the wrapper to the wastebasket.

10. Throw it away.

11. Put the pack of gum away.

A HIDING GAME

1. We're going to play a game.

2. Mary, close your eyes.

3. Don't open them.

4. John, hide the _____ .

5. Mary, open your eyes.

6. Get up.

7. Look for the _____ .

     Colder. Warmer! HOT!

8. (Mary says:) "Oh, here it is!"

9. Good! You found it!

VITAMIN PILL

1. You're going to take your vitamins.

2. Pick up the bottle of vitamin pills.

3. Take the top off.

4. Take out a pill.

5. Put the top back on.

6. Put the bottle down.

7. Put the pill in your mouth.

8. Drink some water and swallow the pill.

9. Uh-oh! It's stuck in your throat!

10. Drink some more water.

11. OK. Good. It went down.

SHARPENING YOUR PENCIL

1. Pick up your pencil.

2. Look at the point.

3. Feel it with your thumb. It's dull.

4. Want to borrow my pencil sharpener?

5. Stick the pencil in the hole.

6. Sharpen the pencil.

pencil
sharpener

7. Feel the point again. Ouch! It's sharp.

8. Clean the pencil sharpener.

9. Give it back to me.

dull

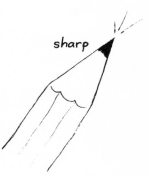

sharp

10. Write a letter.

BREAKFAST CEREAL

1. You're going to eat some cereal for breakfast.

2. Open the box.

3. Pour some cereal in your bowl.

4. Spill some of it on your plate.

5. Pick it up and put it in the bowl.

6. Close the cereal box.

7. Sprinkle some sugar over the cereal.

8. Pour on some milk.

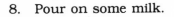

9. Take a bite.

10. Chew it up.

11. Swallow it.

SHOPPING FOR A COAT

1. You're going to go shopping for a new coat.

2. Look in the store windows.

3. Oh! There's a nice coat! Go inside.

4. Take a coat off the rack.

5. Take it off the hanger.

6. Try it on.

7. Look at yourself in the mirror.

8. It's too big. Take it off.

9. Put it back on the hanger.

10. Hang it up.

11. Try on another one.

12. This one fits.

13. Look at the price tag.

14. How much is it?

15. Buy it.

A GLASS OF MILK

1. Pour yourself a glass of milk.

2. Spill some of it on the table.

   Woops!

3. Go to the sink.

4. Pick up a rag.

5. Get it wet.

6. Wring it out.

7. Go back and wipe up the milk.

8. Go back to the sink.

9. Rinse out the rag.

10. Hang it on the faucet.

11. Go back to the table where the milk is.

12. Drink your milk.

13. Be careful. Don't spill any more.

WRAPPING A PRESENT

1. You're going to wrap a present for a friend.

2. Wrap _____ in some tissue paper.

3. Put it in a box.

4. Put the box on some wrapping paper.

5. Wrap it up.

6. Fold the ends.

7. Take two pieces of tape.

8. Tape the ends of the package.

9. Cut a piece of ribbon.

10. Wrap it around the package.

11. Tie a knot.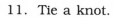

12. Make a bow.

13. Give it to your friend.

"Thank you!"

GOOD MORNING

1. It's seven o'clock in the morning.

2. Wake up.

3. Stretch and yawn and rub your eyes.

4. Get up.

5. Do your exercises.

6. Go to the bathroom.

7. Wash your face.

8. Go back to your bedroom.

9. Get dressed.

10. Make the bed.

11. Go to the kitchen.

12. Eat breakfast.

13. Read the newspaper.

14. Go to the bathroom and brush your teeth.

toothbrush

15. Put on your coat.

16. Kiss your family goodbye.

17. Leave the house.

YOU'RE GETTING SICK

1. You don't feel well.

2. Cover your nose and sneeze.

3. Take out your handkerchief.

4. Blow your nose.

5. Wipe your eyes.

6. Cover your mouth and cough.

7. Leave the house.

8. Go to the drugstore.

9. Oh, you're very weak! Fall down.

10. Get up.

11. Go into the drugstore.

12. Buy some aspirin, kleenex and nasal spray.

13. Go home and take care of yourself.

 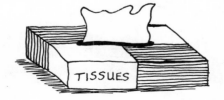

OFFICE WORKER

1. You're a man working in an office.

2. Sit at your desk.

3. Relax.

4. Loosen your tie.

5. Unbutton your jacket.

6. Take it off.

7. Roll up your sleeves.

8. Untie your shoes.

9. Uh-oh! Here comes the boss!

10. Tighten your tie.

11. Put on your jacket.

12. Button it up.

13. Tie your shoes.

14. Get to work.

15. Say hello to the boss.

SEWING ON A BUTTON

1. You're going to sew on a button.

2. Cut a piece of thread.

3. Thread the needle.

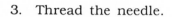

thread

4. Tie a knot at the end.

5. Stick the needle through the cloth.

6. Put it through a hole in the button.

7. Put it through the other hole.

hole

8. Stick it back through the cloth.

9. Pull it tight.

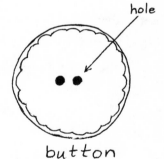

10. Make several more stitches.

button

11. To finish it, stick the needle through the loop.

12. Pull the thread tight.

13. Bite it off.

PAINTING A PICTURE

1. You're going to paint a picture.

2. Spread out some old newspapers.

3. Take out a piece of paper.

4. Open the jar of yellow paint.

5. Pick up the paintbrush.

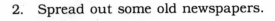

6. Dip it in the paint.

7. Paint a _____ .

8. Let it dry.

9. Close the jar of paint and put it away.

10. Wash the paint out of the brush.

11. Wipe it dry on a rag.

12. Hang the painting on the wall.

13. Fold up the newspapers.

14. Put them away.

TAKING THE PLANE

1. You're going to Hawaii.

2. Get on the plane.

3. Look for your seat number.

4. Sit down.

5. Fasten your seat belt.

6. It's too tight.

7. Loosen it.

8. That's too loose.

9. Tighten it.

10. OK. Here we go!

11. We're taking off.

12. Now we're flying through the air.

13. Unfasten your seat belt.

14. Are you comfortable?   (Yes, I am.)

15. Enjoy your flight.

PLAYING A CASSETTE

1. I want you to hear this song. It's great.

2. Turn on the radio.

3. Switch to *tape*.

4. Press *stop/eject*.

5. Stick the cassette in.

6. Press *play*.

7. Oh, no. That's not it. *Fast-forward* it.

8. OK, hit *play* again.

9. Oh, no. It's on the other side.

10. Push *stop/eject* and then push it again.

11. Take the tape out.

12. Turn it over.

13. Put it back in.

14. *Rewind* it.

15. OK, try it here.

16. Oh, good, this is it. Listen to this.

17. I love this song! Do you want me to *record* it for you?

RESTAURANT

1. You're going out for dinner.

2. Walk into a restaurant.

3. Find a table that's not occupied.

4. Sit down.

5. Pick up the menu and look for something good.

6. Oh, here comes the waitress.

7. Order steak, rice and salad.

8. Unfold your napkin.

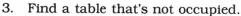

9. Put it in your lap.

10. Take a sip of water.

11. Here comes the food!

12. Enjoy your meal.

OPENING A PRESENT

1. You got a present from your friend!

2. Look it over.

3. Feel it.

4. Shake it and listen to it.

5. Guess what's inside.

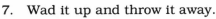

6. Tear off the paper.

7. Wad it up and throw it away.

8. Open the box just a little.

9. Peek inside.

10. Wow! It's just what you wanted!

11. Open the box and take it out.

12. Say, "Oh, thank you!"

A WRINKLED SHIRT

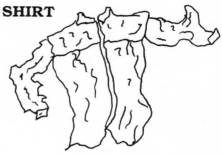

1. Your shirt is wrinkled.

2. You better iron it.

3. Set up the ironing board.

4. Get out the iron.

5. Set it on the ironing board.

6. Plug it in.

7. Turn it on.

8. Wait for it to get hot.

9. Lay your shirt on the ironing board.

10. Spray it with water.

11. Is the iron hot yet?

12. OK. Iron the collar.

13. Now iron the cuffs.

14. Iron the sleeves next.

15. Now iron the rest of the shirt.

16. Finished?

17. Put it on.

18. It looks nice. No more wrinkles.

19. Good job!

ICE CREAM AND TV

1. Go to the refrigerator.

2. Open the freezer.

3. Get the ice cream out.

4. Close the freezer.

5. Put two scoops of ice cream in a bowl.

6. Leave the carton on the counter.

7. Take the ice cream into the other room.

8. Find the remote control.

9. Turn on the TV.

10. Sit down and watch your favorite program.

11. Eat your ice cream.

12. When you're finished, go back for more.

13. Oh no! The ice cream's melted! You forgot to put it away! What a mess!

TAKING CARE OF A BABY

1. You're going to take care of a baby.

2. Hold the baby on your lap.

3. Oh, what a cute baby!

4. Is that a girl or a boy?

5. Kiss him. / her.

6. Hug him. / her.

7. Squeeze him. / her.

8. Offer him / her some cereal.

9. Feed him / her a lot.

10. Oh look! She's / He's spitting it out!

11. Ugh! What a mess!

12. Put him / her down and clean up the mess.

13. What a messy baby!

A BROKEN GLASS

CRASH!

1. Darn! You broke a glass.

2. Pick up the big pieces.

3. Be careful! Don't cut yourself!

4. Take them over to the garbage can.

5. Throw them away.

6. Go get the dustpan and the broom.

7. Go back to the place where you dropped the glass.

8. Lean over and sweep the small pieces into the dustpan.

9. Dump them into the garbage.

10. Put away the dustpan and the broom.

11. Go get another glass.

12. Careful now! Don't drop this one!

TO THE MOON AND BACK

1. Your hand is a rocket.

2. Your other hand is the moon.

3. Your lap is the Earth.

4. Take off.

5. Fly to the moon.

6. Fly around the moon.

7. Land on the moon.

8. Take off.

9. Fly back to Earth.

10. Try to land on Earth.

11. Uh-oh! Something's wrong!

12. The rocket is falling.

13. Crash in the desert.

LET'S PLAY BALL

1. Hey! (John)! Catch!

2. Nice catch!

3. Throw me the ball.

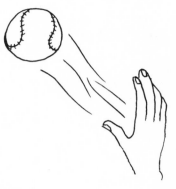

4. Oops! I dropped it.

5. Here, catch!

6. OK, now bounce it on the floor.

7. Bounce it against the wall.

8. Try to catch it.

9. Aw! You missed it. Go get it.

10. Throw it up in the air.

11. Roll it to me.

12. Here you go! Good catch!

13. Now kick it to me.

14. Thanks. I've got to go home now. Bye.

15. Oh, by the way, want to play ball again tomorrow?

HICCUPS

1. You have the hiccups.

2. Do you want to get rid of them?

3. Take a deep breath.

4. Hold your breath.

5. Count to twenty on your fingers.

6. Let your breath out.

7. Are they gone?

8. Fill a glass with water.

9. Drink all of it without stopping.

10. Are they gone yet?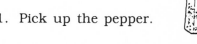

11. Pick up the pepper.

12. Shake a little pepper into the palm of your hand.

13. Breathe it in through your nose.

14. Sneeze.

15. Are they gone yet?

16. Turn around.

17. Close your eyes.

18. BOO!

19. Are they gone now?

USING A PAY PHONE

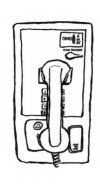

1. You're going to make a phone call.

2. Find a pay phone.

3. Check the coin return.

   ("Nothing!")

4. Pick up the receiver.

5. Take out the correct change.

6. Stick it in the slot.

7. Listen for the dial tone...Do you hear it?

8. Dial the number.

9. It's busy. Hang up.

10. Get your money back.

11. Wait a few minutes.

12. Whistle a tune.

13. Try again.

14. O.K. Good. It's ringing.

15. Talk to your friend.

SOUP FOR LUNCH

1. You're going to heat up some soup for lunch.

2. Pick up the can opener.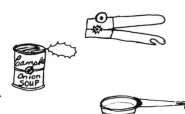

3. Open the can.

4. Pour the soup into a pan.

5. Add one can of water.

6. Stir it up.

7. Put it on the stove.

8. Cover it.

9. Turn on the stove.

10. Wait for the soup to heat up.

11. Take off the lid and check it.

12. It's ready. Turn off the heat.

13. Pour some soup into your bowl.

14. Take a sip.

15. It's too hot! Blow on it.

16. Wait for it to cool off.

17. OK. Now try it again. Ah! Perfect!

CHANGING A LIGHT BULB

1. Turn on the light. It's burned out!

2. You have to change the light bulb.

3. Go get a new one.

4. Unplug the lamp.

5. Take off the lampshade.

6. Unscrew the old bulb.

7. Screw the new one into the socket.

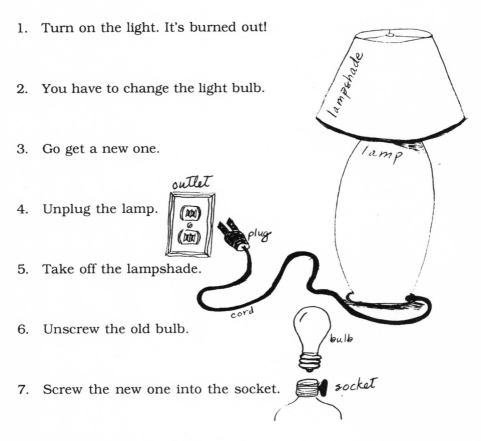

8. Put the lampshade back on.

9. Plug in the lamp.

10. Turn it on. It works!

11. Throw the old bulb away.

BLOODY KNEE

1. You're walking down the street.

2. Fall down and skin your knee and scream.

3. Get up.

4. Cry. It hurts.

5. Look at your knee. It's bleeding!

6. Put your handkerchief on it.

7. Limp to the drugstore.

8. Buy a tube of antibiotic ointment and some bandaids.

9. Limp home.

10. Wash the wound.

11. Ow! It stings! Blow on it.

12. Put some ointment on it. Ah! That feels better.

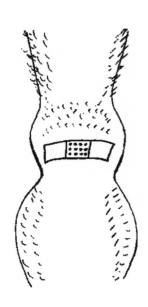

13. Unwrap a bandaid.

14. Put it over the wound.

15. Throw away the wrapper.

SCRAMBLED EGGS

1. You're going to fix scrambled eggs for breakfast.

2. Break three eggs and drop them into a bowl.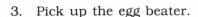

3. Pick up the egg beater.

4. Beat the eggs.

5. Add some salt and a little milk.

6. Mix it with a spoon.

7. Oil the pan.

8. Put it on the stove to heat it up.

9. Pour the egg mixture into the pan.

10. Cook it.

11. Keep stirring it.

12. When it's almost dry, turn off the heat.

13. Put the eggs on a plate and eat them.

BANK

You will find a
check on page 68.

1. You need to cash a check.

2. Walk into the bank.

3. Go over to a counter and write a check.

4. Sign it at the bottom.

5. Go get in line.

6. Wait in line.

7. Move up.

8. Walk up to the window.

9. Hand the check to the teller.

10. Say, "I want to cash this check."

11. Wait a couple of minutes.

12. Take the cash.

13. Count it.

14. Put it away.

15. Go out the door.

A BROKEN PLATE

1. Uh-oh! You broke a plate. You better fix it.

2. Pick up all the pieces.

3. Go get the glue.

4. Unscrew the top.

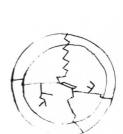

5. Squeeze the tube.

6. Put some glue on the broken edges.

7. Stick the pieces together.

8. Hold it tight for a few minutes.

9. Put it down carefully.

10. Screw the top back on the glue.

11. Put the glue away.

12. Let the glued plate dry overnight.

13. Great! You fixed it!

A MAGIC TRICK

1. You're going to do a magic trick.

2. Fill a glass with water.

3. Dip a piece of string in the water to get it wet.

4. Roll it in salt.

5. Put an ice cube in the glass of water.

6. Sprinkle salt on top of it.

7. Hold up one end of the string.

8. Lay the other end on the ice cube.

9. Wait a minute.

10. Say the magic word: "Abracadabra!"

11. Pull up the string.

12. Wow! Isn't that amazing?

13. You're a great magician!

WRITING A LETTER

1. You're going to write a letter to a friend.

2. Write the date in the upper right-hand corner.

3. Write the letter.

4. Sign your name at the bottom.

5. Fold up the letter.

6. Put it in an envelope.

7. Lick the flap and seal the envelope.

8. Write your friend's name and address on the envelope.

9. Write your own name and address in the upper left-hand corner.

10. Tear off a stamp.

11. Lick it.

12. Stick it in the upper right-hand corner.

13. Take the letter to a mailbox.

14. Mail it.

GOING TO THE MOVIES

1. Go to the movie theater.

2. Buy a ticket.

3. Give it to the ticket-taker at the door.

4. Go into the lobby.

5. Buy some popcorn and something to drink.

6. Go into the theater.

7. Look for a good seat. Here's one. Sit down.

8. Watch the movie and smile.

9. Oh, this part is sad. Cry.

10. Wipe your eyes.

11. This part is scary. Open your eyes wide and scream.

12. This part is funny. Laugh.

13. Now the movie is over. Clap.

14. Get up and leave.

15. How did you like it.?

MAKING A GROCERY LIST

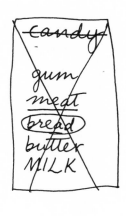

1. Make a list of groceries that you need.

2. Don't forget butter.

3. Erase *sugar*. You have enough sugar.

4. Cross out *candy*. You don't need candy.

5. Underline *meat* so that you won't forget it.

6. Circle *bread*. That's important.

7. Print *MILK* in big letters.

8. What a messy list.

9. Start over.

10. List only the things you really need.

11. That's better.

12. Cross out the first list.

13. Take your list to the grocery store.

14. Don't forget your money.

GROCERY SHOPPING

cart

1. You're in the grocery store.

2. Go to the produce section.

3. Choose some fruit.

4. Put it in your cart.

5. Choose some vegetables.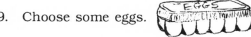

6. Weigh them.

7. That's too much. Put some back.

scale

8. Go to the dairy section.

9. Choose some eggs.

10. That's enough food. Go to the check-out counter.

11. Stand in line.
line

12. Say hello to the cashier.

13. Pay her/him for your groceries.

14. Wait for her/him to bag them.

bag

15. Pick up your bag of groceries and go home.

GIVING DIRECTIONS

1. Let's go to _____'s house.

2. Do you want to drive? I'll sit in the passenger seat.

3. It's that way. Turn around.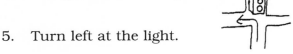

4. Go up there to the light.

5. Turn left at the light.

6. Get on the freeway just past that sign.

7. I think it's the second exit. There it is—Carlson Boulevard. Get off here.

8. Go straight ahead for three blocks.

9. Turn right at the stop sign.

10. Hey, slow down.

11. Go up the hill. It's near the top.

12. Oh! We passed it. Back up.

13. Here it is. Look. It's across the street from the school.

14. OK, park here.

HAIRCUT

1. Your hair is getting long. You need a haircut.

2. Go to the barbershop.

3. The barber's busy.

4. Have a seat and wait your turn.

5. Read a magazine while you wait.

"Next!"

6. Get up.

7. Go sit in the barber's chair.

8. Chat with the barber.

9. Watch her/him in the mirror while she/he works.

10. OK. All done. Look at yourself in the mirror.

11. You look great! Get up.

12. Pay the barber.

13. What a terrific barber! Give her/him a tip.

EATING ORANGES

1. There are three ways to eat an orange.

2. Here's the first way:

3. Peel it.

4. Pull it apart.

1

5. Take out the seeds.

6. Eat each section.

7. Here's the second way:

8. Cut it in half, then in quarters and then in eighths.

2

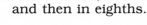

9. Bite the pulp off the peel.

10. Spit out the seeds.

11. Here's the third way:

3

12. Roll it between your hands.

13. Cut a hole in one end.

14. Squeeze the orange.

15. Suck out the juice.

RAINY DAY

1. You're walking in the rain.

2. Stop. There's a big puddle.

3. Step over it.

4. Oh! It stopped raining. Close your umbrella.

5. Start running.

6. Be careful! There's some mud!

7. Slip in the mud.

8. Fall down.

9. Get up and look at yourself. You're all muddy!

10. Go back to the puddle.

11. Step in it.

12. Stamp your foot. (Splash!)

13. Jump up and down.

14. Get out of that puddle!

15. Look at you! You're all wet!

16. Go home and change your clothes.

A ROUGH BUS RIDE

1. You're waiting for the bus.

2. Oh! Here it comes!

3. Get on.

4. Pay the driver.

5. Ask for a transfer.

6. Gosh! This driver is terrible! Fall down!

7. Get up.

8. Tell the driver to take it easy.

9. Sit down. Look out the window.

10. Bounce up and down.

11. Watch for your street.

12. There it is! Ring the bell.

13. Don't stand up until the bus stops.

14. OK. Now stand up and go to the back door.

15. Step down.

16. Push the door open.

17. Get off the bus.

18. Wipe your forehead and say,
    "Whew! What a ride!"

BUILDING A FIRE

1. Brrr! It's cold! Let's build a fire.

2. Take your ax out to the woods.

3. Chop down a dead tree.

4. Chop off a log.

5. Carry the log inside.

6. Set it down next to the fireplace.

7. Put some paper in your fireplace.

8. Put some small sticks on top of the paper.

9. Lay the log on top of the sticks.

10. Light a match.

11. Light the paper to start the fire.

12. Blow on it.

13. Fan it. Good! It's burning.

14. Sit in your rocking chair.

15. Rock back and forth.

16. Watch the fire. Beautiful! Fascinating!

17. Fall asleep in front of the fire.

GOING SWIMMING

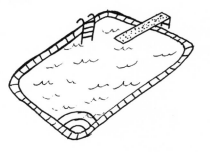

1. You're going to go swimming.

2. Put on your swim suit.

3. Stand at the edge of the pool.

4. Hold your nose.

5. Take a deep breath.

6. Jump in. (Splash!)

7. Swim across the pool.

8. Climb up the ladder and get out.

9. Go to the diving board.

10. Walk out over the water.

11. Dive into the water. Beautiful!

12. Swim underwater.

13. Hold your breath!

14. Swim to the surface.

15. Hold on to the edge.

16. Breathe hard.

17. Splash your friend.

A PIECE OF TOAST

1. You're going to eat a piece of toast.

2. Take out a slice of bread.

3. Put it in the toaster.

4. Push the lever down.

5. Wait a minute.

6. It's done!

7. Take out the toast and put it on your plate.

8. Spread some butter on it.

9. Watch it melt in.

10. Put a spoonful of jam on the toast.

11. Spread it around with a knife.

12. Cut the toast in half.

13. Pick up one half.

14. Try it.

15. Is it good?

16. Eat it all.

A BIRD

1. You're a bird in a tree.

2. Flap your wings.

3. Fly through the air.

4. Land on the ground.

5. Hop around.

6. Look for bugs.

7. You found one! Carry it in your beak.

8. Fly back to the tree.

9. Swallow the bug.

10. Sing to another bird.

11. Build a nest.

12. Sit in the nest.

13. Clean your feathers.

14. Lay an egg.

A BEAUTIFUL DAY

1. What a beautiful sunny day!

2. Sigh and go outside.

3. Stretch and yawn.

4. Lie down in the sun.

5. Oh, it's too hot!

6. You're sweating.

7. Sit up and look for a shady place.

8. Ah! There's a big shady tree.

9. Walk over to it.

10. Sit down in the shade.

11. Oh, it's nice and cool here.

12. Sigh and stretch and yawn again.

13. Lie down in the shade.

14. Go to sleep.

A PARTY!

1. You're having a party.

2. Put on some music.

3. Introduce two of your guests to each other.

4. Here comes another guest. Wave to her/him and shout "Hello!"

5. Offer some chips to some of your guests.

6. Eat some yourself.

7. Take a sip of your drink.

8. Clap your hands to the music.

9. Snap your fingers.

10. Tap your foot.

11. Nod your head.

12. Ask someone to dance with you.

13. Move your whole body to the music.

14. Face your partner.

15. Wink at him./her.

16. Are you having a good time?

17. Me too. This is a great party!

TIME TO CLEAN HOUSE

1. Boy, your house sure is dirty!

2. Put on your apron.

3. Sprinkle some kitchen cleanser in the sink.

4. Scrub the sink with a sponge.

5. Sweep the kitchen floor with a broom.

6. Fill a bucket with water.

7. Pour some liquid cleaner in it.

8. Stick the mop in it.

9. Mop the kitchen floor.

10. Dust the furniture with a dust cloth.

11. Empty the wastebaskets.

12. Plug in the vacuum cleaner.

13. Turn it on.

14. Vacuum the rugs and carpets.

15. Put all the cleaning stuff away.

16. Look around. It looks much better!

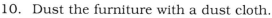

SPEEDING

1. You're going to take a ride in your car.

2. Take out your car key.

3. Unlock the car door.

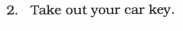

4. Open it.

5. Get in.

6. Fasten your seatbelt.

7. Start the engine.

8. Release the hand brake.

9. Put the car in first gear.

10. Drive away.

11. Change to second gear.

12. Speed up.

13. Shift into third.

14. Uh-oh! Too fast! Here comes a policeman.

15. Pull over to the side of the street and stop.

16. Roll down the window.

17. Say, "I'm sorry, officer."

18. Start to cry.

19. That did it! He's not going to give you a ticket—this time.

DOG

1. You're a dog.

2. Here comes a cat!

3. Chase it!

4. It ran up a tree. Bark at it.

5. It's no use. Look for something else to do.

6. Sniff the ground.

7. There's an old bone! Chew on it.

8. Take it to the vegetable garden.

9. Dig a hole with your paws.

10. Bury the bone.

11. Here comes your master! Wag your tail.

12. Uh-oh! He's mad at you for digging a hole.

13. Hang your head. Aren't you ashamed?

14. Sit in the corner. What a naughty dog!

A MAN GETTING READY TO GO OUT

1. It's Saturday night and you're going to go out with your girlfriend.

2. Shave.

3. Clip your nails.

4. Take a shower.

5. Wash your hair.

6. Dry yourself.

7. Put on some cologne.

8. Get dressed.

9. Look at yourself in the mirror.

10. Comb your hair.

11. You look good.

12. Go borrow some money from your friend.

13. Buy some flowers.

14. Go pick up your girl.

15. Have a good time!

A WOMAN GETTING READY FOR A DATE

1. It's Saturday night and you're going to go out with your boyfriend.

2. File your nails.

3. Take a bubble bath.

4. Soak for a long time.

5. Shave your legs.

6. Get out of the tub.

7. Dry yourself.

8. Powder yourself.

9. Put on some perfume.

10. Get dressed.

11. Look at yourself in the mirror.

12. Fix your hair.

13. Put some fingernail polish on.

14. Put on your make-up.

15. You look beautiful! Wait for him to pick you up.

16. Have a great time!

AT THE LAUNDROMAT

1. You're going to do your laundry at a laundromat.

2. Sort your clothes into two piles.

3. Put the dark ones in one machine and the light ones in another.

4. Add half a cup of detergent to each load.

5. Set the water temperature.

6. Put some coins in the slot of each machine.

7. Sit down and wait for the machines to finish.

8. When they're finished, take out your clothes.

9. Put them in a dryer.

10. Set it on medium heat.

11. Put some coins in the slot.

12. Wait for the dryer to finish.

13. When it's finished, take out your clothes.

14. Sort them.

15. Fold them up.

DOCTOR'S APPOINTMENT

1. You have a doctor's appointment.

2. Go to the doctor's office.

3. Tell the receptionist your name.

4. Tell her/him what time your appointment is.

5. Have a seat.

6. You're nervous. Sit on the edge of your chair.

7. Bite your fingernails.

8. Wait for half an hour.

9. Finally! Here comes the nurse.

10. Follow him/her into the examination room.

11. Say hello to the doctor.

12. Sit down.

13. Open your mouth wide.

14. Stick out your tongue and say, "Ah."

15. You're fine! Say goodbye to the doctor.

16. Ask the receptionist how much you have to pay.

PUTTING DROPS IN YOUR EYES

1. You're going to put drops in your eyes.

2. Open the bottle of eye drops.

3. Put your head back.

4. Open your eyes wide.

5. Keep them open.

6. Hold one eye open with your fingers.

7. Squeeze a drop into it.

8. Don't blink!

9. Oh! You missed! The drop is running down your cheek.

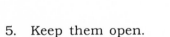

10. Wipe it off.

11. Try again.

12. There! That's it. You did it.

13. Go ahead and blink now.

PUTTING UP A TOWEL RACK

1. You're going to put up a towel rack in the bathroom.

2. Hold the towel rack where you want to put it up.

3. Make four marks on the wall where the holes are.

4. Put the towel rack down.

5. Make four holes in the wall where the marks are.

6. Hold up the towel rack again.

7. Stick a screw in one hole.

   screw

8. Screw it in part way.

9. Screw the other screws in part way.

   screwdriver

10. OK. Now all the screws are in, but they're all loose.

11. Tighten them with a screwdriver. All the way in.

12. Great! They're all tight! Where are the towels?

CASHIER

You will find a check, a
credit card and a driver's
license on page 68.

1. You're a cashier.

2. A customer wants you to change a ten-dollar bill.

3. Take the ten.

4. Give him her the change as you count it.

5. Another customer wants to cash a check.

6. Ask him her for his her ID:

   "May I see your driver's license and a credit card?"

7. Look at his her driver's license.

8. On the back of the check, copy the license number and the date of birth.

9. Look at his her credit card.

10. Write down the name of the company and the number of the credit card.

11. Count the cash as you give it to the customer.

TAKING PICTURES

1. You're going to take some pictures of your friends.

2. Tell your friends where to stand:
   "Please stand over there."

3. Hold up your camera and look at the screen.

4. Tell them to stand closer together:
   "Please stand closer together."

5. Tell them to spread out.

6. Tell (Peter) to sit down.

7. Tell John to move over.

8. Tell (Joan) to get in front of (Sarah).

9. Tell (Bill) to get behind (Tom).

10. Tell everybody to smile.

11. Press the button.

12. Tell them all to stay where they are:
    "Stay where you are."

13. Take another picture.

MAKING A TABLE

1. You're going to make a table.

2. Choose a nice board.

3. Take out your tape measure.

4. Measure the board.

5. Mark it where you want to cut it.

6. Pick up your saw.

7. Saw through the board.

8. Take out your hammer and four nails.

9. Hold a nail in one hand and your hammer in the other.

10. Pound the nail into the board.

11. Pound the other nails into the other corners.

12. Turn it over.

13. Hey, that's a nice table!

14. You're a great carpenter!

TAKING A HIKE

1. You're going to go on a hike in the mountains.

2. Start climbing up the mountain.

3. You're getting thirsty.

4. Stop and have a drink of water.

5. OK. Go ahead.

6. You're starting to get tired. You're out of breath.

7. Sit down and catch your breath.

8. All right. Get up and get going.

9. Now you're getting hungry.

10. Stop and eat an apple.

11. Hike all the way to the top of the mountain.

12. Oh! Look! What a beautiful view!

13. Are you tired? Are you thirsty? Are you out of breath? Are you hungry?

14. Sit down and rest.

15. Drink some more water and have a snack.

16. Relax for a while.

17. OK. Ready? Come on. Get up.

18. Climb down the mountain.

19. What a great way to spend the day!

BOO! OCT. 31

A JACK-O-LANTERN FOR HALLOWEEN

1. You're going to carve a pumpkin for Halloween.

2. Cut a circle in the top of the pumpkin.

3. Take it off.

4. Cut off the pulp.

5. Clean out the pumpkin with a big spoon.

6. Cut out two eyes and a nose.

7. Cut out a big scary grin.

8. Light a short candle.

9. Wait for the wax to melt.

10. Drip some wax in the bottom of the pumpkin.

11. Stick the candle in the melted wax.

12. Put the top on.

13. Put the jack-o-lantern in the window.

14. Clean up the mess.

A THANKSGIVING FEAST

1. You're going to have a Thanksgiving feast.

2. Set the table.

3. Take the roast turkey out of the oven.

4. Put all the food on the table.

5. Call your family to the table:
   "It's time to eat!"

6. Sit down.

7. Say grace.

8. Carve the turkey.

9. Serve some to each person.

10. Pass the rest of the food around the table.

11. Eat a lot.

12. Say, "I'm full!"

68

You have our permission to make copies of this page so that students can cut out the items for use with "Bank" (p. 35) and "Cashier" (p. 62). Or copy your own credit card, driver's license and check.

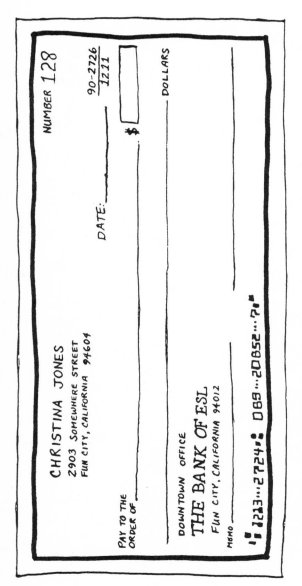

LIST OF PROPS FOR EACH LESSON

R — real   **P** — picture (photograph or drawing)

1. *Washing Your Hands*: soap, towel, towel rack (loose or fixed), faucet (R, P, plastic, or drawing on board with erasable water!)

2. *Candle*: candle, candle holder, matchbook; *class sets of* : birthday cake candles, cake candle holders, matchbooks for everyone

3. *Getting Home*: home (P(s)), stairway (R or P), keyhole (R or P), doorknob (R or P), key, door lock (R or P)

4. *Cheese*: wrapped cheese, cutting board, knife

5. *Balloon*: *class set* of balloons (have students initial them in ink when inflated so that they can be retrieved after they are flown)

6. *Chewing Gum*: store (P or group of items "for sale" on table), gum (several unopened packs)

7. *A Hiding Game*: small objects (can be props from other lessons)

8. *Vitamin Pill*: vitamin bottle, candy "pills"

9. *Sharpening Your Pencil*: dull pencil, hand-held pencil sharpener (preferably one that is not disguised as something else)

10. *Breakfast Cereal*: box of cold cereal, bowl, plate (can be paper), sugar bowl with sugar, milk carton, spoon

11. *Shopping for a Coat*: store windows (P or imaginary), rack (any kind; an over-the-door rack is simple to transport), hangers (several), coats (yours and/or students'), price tags (on each coat, handmade or from a store)

12. *A Glass of Milk*: glass (can be clear plastic), milk carton (filled with water), rag (raggedy), sink (R or P)

13. *Wrapping a Present*: boxes of various sizes (and colors?), tissue paper and gift wrap (several pieces of new or used each; also can be of different colors), cellophane tape (several rolls if possible), ribbon (several spools if possible, of different colors; you may also bring in pieces of cloth ribbon— velvet and satin—to introduce such words), presents (any objects you have on hand), scissors

14. *Good Morning*: clock (R or cardboard or P), bed (can be a chair with a pillow and small blanket), bathroom (designated area of the room with a few toiletries or a P), kitchen (designated area of the room with a breakfast table setting or a P), newspaper, toothbrush, coat, family (P or imaginary; or performer can blow or give pretend kisses to two or three students or to the whole class)

R — real   **P** — picture (photograph or drawing)

15. *You're Getting Sick*: handkerchief (*not* tissue), drugstore (P or designated area of class with several pharmaceutical items), aspirin, kleenex, nasal spray bottle

16. *Office Worker*: tie (not clip-on), jacket (blazer-type), long-sleeved shirt

17. *Sewing on a Button*: very large button with 2 holes, spool of thread, scissors, needle (the larger the better for visibility), old shirt

18. *Painting a Picture*: old newspapers, set of paints (small poster temperas from supermarket—not solid watercolors), rag, paintbrush, jar of water, white paper, tape or thumbtacks (to hang picture on wall)

19. *Taking the Plane*: plane (P), seat belt (any kind of adjustable belt will do)

20. *Playing a Cassette*: cassette with a nice, easy song; radio/cassette player with all functions in lesson (radio/tape switch, stop/eject button, fast-forward, rewind, play and record buttons); use illustration on p. 20 for pair practice

21. *Restaurant*: restaurant (P), fork, knife, spoon, napkin (cloth or paper), menu (R or folder or piece of paper labeled "Menu")

22. *Opening a Present*: presents (several objects wrapped in boxes but without tissue inside—use familiar props from the class if you aren't prepared to be actually giving things to the students)

23. *A Wrinkled Shirt*: 2 long-sleeved shirts (one wrinkled, the other not), ironing board (or any wooden board), iron with cord (R, or use any object that can be set on end and can also be laid down, such as a stapler), spray bottle with water

24. *Ice Cream and TV*: combination refrigerator and freezer (storage cabinet or bookcase or P), ice cream (empty ice cream carton of any shape), scoop, bowl, spoon, counter (or table), remote control, TV (R, box or P)

25. *Taking Care of a Baby*: baby (large doll or anything, especially if wrapped in a blanket), cup, spoon

26. *A Broken Glass*: broken glass (clear plastic tumbler, cut up), garbage can (or wastebasket—check that it's not too dirty—you want to retrieve your broken pieces after each performance of the sequence), dustpan, broom (or whisk broom), another glass (plastic or glass)

27. *To the Moon and Back*: P's of rocket, earth, moon, desert (for clarification only, not as props to use in performance

R — real   **P** — picture (photograph or drawing)

28. *Let's Play Ball*: ball (or class set of "superballs" or other balls, especially very bouncy ones)

29. *Hiccups*: container of drinking water, glass, pepper shaker full of pepper

30. *Using a Pay Phone*: pay phone (R or plastic toy phone housed in a shoe box to which you have added a slot and a coin return)

31. *Soup for Lunch*: can opener (hand-held type), soup can, saucepan with lid, spoon, stove (R, P or a book), bowl

32. *Changing a Light Bulb*: small lamp with removable shade, burnt-out bulb, good bulb

33. *Bloody Knee*: handkerchief (cloth or tissue with red stains), tube of antibiotic ointment, bandaids, drugstore (see #15)

34. *Scrambled Eggs*: plastic Easter eggs that open, bowl, egg beater, spoon, salt shaker, milk (carton), oil (bottle), pan, stove (R, P or a book), plate, fork

35. *Bank*: bank (P or area of classroom), checks (R or from page 68), cash (R or play)

36. *A Broken Plate*: old plate (R, plastic or paper; can be already broken but not in too many pieces), glue (in a tube)

37. *A Magic Trick*: glass (can be clear plastic); jar, pitcher or bottle of water; string, salt, plate (to roll string in salt), ice cubes

38. *Writing a Letter*: paper, envelopes (students can make them from paper), stamps (from magazine mail order companies), mailbox (P or box with slot)

39. *Going to the Movies*: ticket(s) (optional), popcorn (R, or popcorn box or bag filled with styrofoam puffs if available), drink (empty soda cup), lobby, theater (arrange the room to designate these areas)

40. *Making a Grocery List*: no props needed; make a list on the blackboard

41. *Grocery Shopping*: grocery store with produce and dairy sections and a check-out counter (arrange room; furnish produce section with plastic items and bags, dairy section with empty dairy containers, check-out counter with paper and plastic bags), scale (R, or make a cardboard one with movable dial and pounds and ounces marked), cart (a box in a chair works fine)

R — real   **P** — picture (photograph or drawing)

42. *Giving Directions*: Option 1: draw a map of all these streets, blocks, buildings, stops and signs, and use a small toy car to drive on the map *and/or* Option 2: car (two chairs), steering wheel (R or P or toy or imaginary); stop light (toy or P) and stop sign (toy or P); streets (P), freeway (P), hill (P), school (P); signs: "FREEWAY ENTRANCE," "CARLSON BLVD." and two EXIT signs (because Carlson is "the second exit" according to the lesson) (all signs with arrow)

43. *Haircut*: no scissors! (use your fingers), magazine, mirror (R or imagined or P)

44. *Eating Oranges*: at least 3 oranges (R, with seeds), sharp knife, damp paper towels (to wipe juice off hands)

45. *Rainy Day*: umbrella, puddle (a little water on the floor)

46. *A Rough Bus Ride*: transfer, bus stop (chair), bus (chair arrangement)

47. *Building a Fire*: ax (P), tree (P, chair or podium), log (R only, *not* particleboard), fireplace (defined by hands, or P), sticks (R), newspaper, matches, rocking chair (any chair can be rocked)

48. *Going Swimming*: swimming pool (P), water (optional—in a bowl to demonstrate splashing)

49. *A Piece of Toast*: loaf of sliced bread, toaster, plate, knife, spoon, butter, jam (all R)

50. *A Bird*: bug (plastic), feather (R, to show what it is), nest (your coat or sweater in your chair), egg (preferably a large artificial one, hidden in nest)

51. *A Beautiful Day*: shady tree (P)

52. *A Party*: music, chips, drink

53. *Time to Clean House*: apron, kitchen cleanser, sink (bowl or P), broom, bucket, liquid cleaner, dust cloth, small wastebaskets, vacuum cleaner (R, toy or P), small rug

54. *Speeding*: key, car (chair)

55. *Dog*: bone (R or realistic dog toy)

56. *A Man Getting Ready to Go Out*: razor, nail scissors or clippers, shampoo (optional), towel, cologne (bottle), comb, flowers (artificial)

R — real   **P** — picture (photograph or drawing)

57. *A Woman Getting Ready for a Date*: nail file, bubble bath liquid, tub (P for clarification, chair for use), razor, towel, powder, perfume, nail polish, barrettes (or something for hair), makeup (can use pens)

58. *At the Laundromat*: old clothes, washing machines and dryers (boxes with slots for money and dials for temperature settings), detergent, cup

59. *Doctor's Appointment*: no props

60. *Putting Drops in Your Eyes*: eye drops (water in a dropper bottle)

61. *Putting Up a Towel Rack*: towel rack, screws, screwdriver, bulletin board or other surface on which to install rack

62. *Cashier*: money (R or play), driver's license, credit card, check (from p. 68)

63. *Taking Pictures*: digital camera (or small box)

64. *Making a Table*: boards (small, slightly different ones), tape measure, saw, hammer, nails (gigantic)

65. *Taking a Hike*: canteen (or any object to drink from), apple; *optional* : walking stick (any stick or pole)

66. *A Jack-O-Lantern for Halloween*: pumpkins, big spoons, sharp knives, short candles, newspapers (have the students bring these things)

67. *A Thanksgiving Feast*: plates, knives, forks, spoons, napkins, glasses (or cups), roast turkey (stuffed paper bag), food (plastic)

PAGE CORRESPONDENCES:
Live Action English ➔ *Action English Pictures*

LAE	AEP	LAE	AEP	LAE	AEP	LAE	AEP
1	13	17	38	33	28	49	11
3	16	18	41	34	10	51	104
8	24	19	64	35	61	53	47
9	88	22	70	36	29	58	59
10	9	24	48	38	44	60	26
11	54	25	40	39	78	61	43
12	12	26	30	41	58	63	80
13	76	30	57	43	62	66	72
14	8	31	14	45	103	67	73
15	25	32	42	46	63		

 **LIVE ACTION ENGLISH AUDIO CDs**

Two CDs—a spirited and charming complete reading of all 67 lessons in the book with pauses for student repetition, done in 2000 by co-author Elizabeth Kuizenga. Many enhanced by sound effects. Available from most distributors listed inside the front cover.

LIVE ACTION ENGLISH CD-ROM NOW AVAILABLE!!!

Live Action English Interactive is the first **TPR** computer program ever—a program that amazes and delights. For example, the program tells you, "Put on your sweater." You choose the sweater from a few objects and drag it to the person in the video, who takes it and puts it on. Nine of the 12 units are lessons from the book.

Seven activities in each unit: Watch (the series of actions on video or in still photos; you can do the actions in pantomime as you watch, then without watching), Listen (choose the right frame to match what you hear), Interact (the program tells you what to do, you do it and the appropriate action happens on screen), Watch & Read (the series on video or in stills with the script), Order (drag sentences into the right order), Verbs (practice verb forms of four basic tenses in context in stories) and Write (type sentences after hearing them; hints provided when necessary; the action occurs when the sentence is correct).

High beginning and low intermediate. Grades 3-12, college and adult levels. Windows and Macintosh. See the **demo** at http://www.speakware.com. Available from most distributors listed inside the front cover. *Live Action Spanish Interactive is also available.*

ACTION ENGLISH PICTURES
A GREAT COMPANION FOR LIVE ACTION ENGLISH
and ALL FOREIGN LANGUAGE VERSIONS:

Shown here is "Taking Care of a Baby" from page 25 in *Live Action English*. See description on back cover. Available only from Alta Book Center.

DISTRIBUTORS LISTED INSIDE FRONT COVER